It's a Wild life, buddy!

Daniela De Luca

Buster
the Kangaroo

Tommy
NELSON

D1401945

EARLY ONE MORNING, far away in the Australian outback, Buster got ready to leap into his mother's safe, warm pouch as he always did. But this time, Mother Kangaroo stopped him. "No, Buster. You're a big boy now. And quite soon you will have a new baby sister! She is growing in my pouch right now."

DO BABY KANGAROOS REALLY GROW IN THEIR MOTHERS' POUCHES?

Yes. When kangaroos are born, they are very small and helpless. The tiny creatures clamber into their mothers' pouches where they are safe and warm. They drink milk to help them grow.

HOW LONG DO THEY STAY IN THE POUCH?

For several months, depending on the species. But even after they leave the pouch they still suckle milk and their mothers take care of them.

BUSTER WAS VERY UPSET with his mother and his new baby sister—even though he hadn't even seen her yet. Sadly he remembered when he used to bound across the desert, safely tucked inside his mother's pouch. Buster used to smile and wave at all of his friends in the mob around him.

WHAT IS A MOB?
A mob is a group of 50 or more kangaroos that live together. Not all kangaroos live in mobs, although most of the larger species do.

6

USTER AND HIS MOTHER used to do everything together.
hen the rains came, the dry desert was filled with tender,
een grass and pretty flowers. Buster's mother showed
m which were the best types of leaves to eat.

WHAT DO KANGAROOS EAT?
Most kangaroos eat grass, leaves, roots, seeds, and fruit.
A few of the smaller species also feed on insects.

BUSTER HOPPED ON AND ON, through the bush, over the grasslands, and across the burning red desert. After some time, he began to realize just how large the outback was. "I don't think I'm getting anywhere at all!" he said aloud. But there was no one to hear him. As he met other animals along the way, he would always stop and talk. He was happy to have someone to listen.

Apari Emu

Kadee Emu

Berrinigar and Darel Emu

Jannali Emu

HOW DO KANGAROOS MOVE?
Kangaroos have large, strong hind legs which power them along as they hop through the bush and desert. At full speed, they can travel at more than 35 mph (55 km/h).

BUSTER WAS VERY SAD. He sat and wept. His friends Rob and Tina Wombat tried to comfort him, but there was nothing they could say or do that would cheer him up.

THEN BUSTER HAD AN IDEA.
"If they don't want me here,
then I'll just run away!" he said
to Rob and Tina. So he packed
a few things into his backpack
and skipped off through the
bush at great speed.

Nalong Molloch

Erik Echidna

Tammy
Echidna

13

Kami
Frilled
Lizard

Sir John Marsupial Mouse

12

HOW DO KANGAROOS KEEP CLEAN?
Kangaroos sometimes go in the water, but usually to keep cool rather than to stay clean. They use the claws on their short front legs to remove pests and groom themselves.

AT DUSK, Buster came upon a billabong. There were cockatoos all crowded around chatting and having their evening drink. Buster drank too.

14

ARE KANGAROOS AFRAID OF OTHER ANIMALS?
Apart from humans, the only other animals kangaroos fear are dingos and eagles. Dingos are a type of wild dog that live in Australia (above).

BUSTER WAS VERY TIRED. He snuggled up to a warm rock and groomed himself for a while as playful little bats flew about his head. Just before he fell asleep, Buster decided to go and visit his cousin Grey who lived far away in the acacia forests.

BUSTER SET OFF early the next morning. He soon met a friendly group of koalas who invited him to breakfast in their gum tree house. But as Buster sat sipping h tea, his nose began to twitch. What was that strange smell?

WAS SMOKE! The bush was on fire! All the animals began to leap and
mp—anything to avoid the flames and smoke. Buster scrambled down,
it of the tree, and ran as far away as his little legs could carry him.

WHAT HAPPENS TO THE BUSH AFTER A FIRE?
Bush fires are common in Australia,
and the local trees and plants are hardy.
Normally the fire passes over them quickly,
and only the leaves are burnt. Within a few
months, the bush is fully recovered.

BUSTER AND HIS FRIENDS, Terence and Teresa and their Platypus family, finally reached a stream. Buster hopped into the cool water. Just then, the wind changed, sending the fire off in a new direction. Buster was safe with his new friends.

19

BUSTER SOON SET OUT again. He hopped
through the bush all day, until—suddenly—
he heard loud stomping noises ahead. He
peeped out from behind a tree and saw his
cousin Grey boxing with another kangaroo

"Hi Grey," shouted Buster.
The cousins hugged each other.

"Come on," Grey said.
"Let's go home."

DO KANGAROOS REALLY BOX?
Yes, they do. Male kangaroos
fight each other at mating time.
They stand upright face to face,
then lock arms and try to push
each other backward. This is
known as "boxing."

GREY PUT
HIS ARM
AROUND
BUSTER, and
the two
kangaroos,
giggling and telling
stories, set off for home.

21

HOW DO KANGAROOS TALK TO EACH OTHER?
Kangaroos are not noisy animals. The males hiss and spit while fighting, but otherwise the females just make clicking sounds to call their young.

THE TWO LITTLE KANGAROOS got close to a clearing in the bush, they heard the
cited chatter of the mob. What a surprise! Buster's mother was there waiting for
n, with his baby sister, Chrissy, peeping out of her pouch! Buster smiled at his
w sister, then looked to Mother. "I've explored the whole outback, but my
orite place is right here, with my family." Mother just smiled proudly and
lcomed Buster home with a hug.

23

Virginia Opossums

Wombat

DID YOU KNO
LIKE ALL KANGAROOS, Buster
marsupial. Female marsupials
different from all other animals beca
they have pouches on their stomach
which they carry their babies. M
marsupials live in Australia and N
Zealand. One or two species live in
Americas, mainly in the sou

Numbat

Tasmanian Devil

Rat Kangaroo

Bandicoot

Koala

Honey Possum

Marsupial Mole

Wallaby

25

Flying opossum

Bats

Koala

Eastern Quoll

THIS PICTURE SHOWS Buster pos
with his friends. All these animals l
in Australia, New Zealand, and Pap
New Guinea. Can you see Bust
Do you recognize all his frien

Emu

BUSTER

Platypus

Dingo

Wallaby

Black Swan

Wombat

Molloch

Echidna

Frilled Lizard

Penguir

26

Pink cockatoo

Bird of paradise

Petauro dello zucchero

Flying squirrel

Acrobate pigmeo

Gray kangaroo

Cassowary

Parrot

Echidna

Dasiuro

Kiwi

Tuatara

Crocodile

Marsupial mouse

Tasmanian devil

27

So God made the wild animals, the tame animals and all the small crawling animals. . . . God saw that this was good.
Genesis 1:25

Copyright © 2005 McRae Books Srl, Borgo S. Croce, 8 – Florence, Italy
info@mcraebooks.com

ISBN 1-4003-0605-1

Scripture quoted from the *International Children's Bible®, New Century Version®,* copyright © 1986, 1988, 1999 by Tommy Nelson®, a Division of Thomas Nelson, Inc., Nashville, Tennessee 37214.

This book was conceived, edited and designed by McRae Books Srl, Florence, Italy.

North American version published by Tommy Nelson®, a Division of Thomas Nelson, Inc.

Publishers: Anne McRae, Marco Nardi
Text: Vicky Egan
Illustrations: Daniela De Luca
Designer: Rebecca Milner, Sebastiano Ranchetti

05 06 07 08 09 – 5 4 3 2 1

Repro: Litocolor, Florence, Italy
Printed and bound in China